एक नया
Ek Naya Din
A New Day

Reader's guide

Each page has three sentences about the fun filled day
Reyan is having with his parents.
First line - Hindi in Devanagari script.
Second line - English transliteration for the Hindi sentence.
Third line - English translation of the Hindi Sentence.
For rhyming effect, read the Hindi sentences on each
spread together.

नमस्ते माँ! देखो सूरज निकल आया।
Namaste maa! Dekho, suraj nikal aaya.
Hello Mom! Look, the sun is out.

नमस्ते रेयान! मस्ती भरा नया दिन है लाया।
Namaste Reyan! Masti bhara naya din hai laya.
Hello Reyan! It brings a new day full of fun.

आज नाश्ते में मुझे क्या मिलेगा ?

Aaj nashte mein mujhe kya milega?

What will I get for breakfast today?

गरम आलू पराठे पे मक्खन लगेगा।
Garam aloo parathe pe makhan lagega.
A hot potato flatbread with butter.

आज बाहर चल कर कुछ मज़ेदार करते हैं।
Aaj bahar chal kar kuchh mazedaar karte hain!
Let's go outside and do something fun today!

जल्दी से कपड़े बदल कर, जूते पहनते हैं।

Jaldi se kapde badal kar, joote pahente hain.

Let's quickly change our clothes and wear our shoes.

एक गाड़ी, दो बस, तीन ट्रक, चार पेड़, और पांच चिड़ियाँ।
Ek gadi, do bus, teen truck, chaar ped, aur paanch chidiyan.
One car, two buses, three trucks, four trees and five birds.

चलो, सेब से भरे पेड़ हैं खोजते।

Chalo, seb se bhare ped hain khojte.

Let's go, search for some trees full of apples.

लाल सेब तोड़ते, हरे सेब छोड़ते।

Laal seb todte, hare seb chodte.

Pluck the red apples, leave the green ones.

आज खाने में सांबर के साथ है इडली और वड़ा।

Aaj khane mein sambar ke saath hai idli aur vada.

Today, lunch is lentil curry with rice cakes and lentil fritters.

एक एक कर के खाने से स्वाद और भी बड़ा।

Ek ek kar ke khane se swad aur bhi bada.

Eating them one by one makes them taste even better.

चलो उनको गाजर खिलाते हैं उधर।
Chalo unko gaajar khilaatein hain udhar.
Let's go feed them carrots over there.

यहां लाल, नारंगी, पीले, हरे, नीले और बैंगनी फूलों को देखो ज़रा।

Yahan laal, narangi, peele, hare, neele, aur bainganee phoolon ko dekho zara.

Look at the red, orange, yellow, green, blue, and purple flowers over here.

वहां आसमान में इन्द्रधनुष है सात रंगों से भरा।

Wahan aasmaan mein indradhanush hai saat rangon se bhara.

The sky has a rainbow full of seven colors over there.

गर्मियों में ठंडी ठंडी कुल्फी लगती है अच्छी।
Garmiyon mein thandi thandi kulfi lagti hai achhi.
During summer, cold cold ice cream feels good.

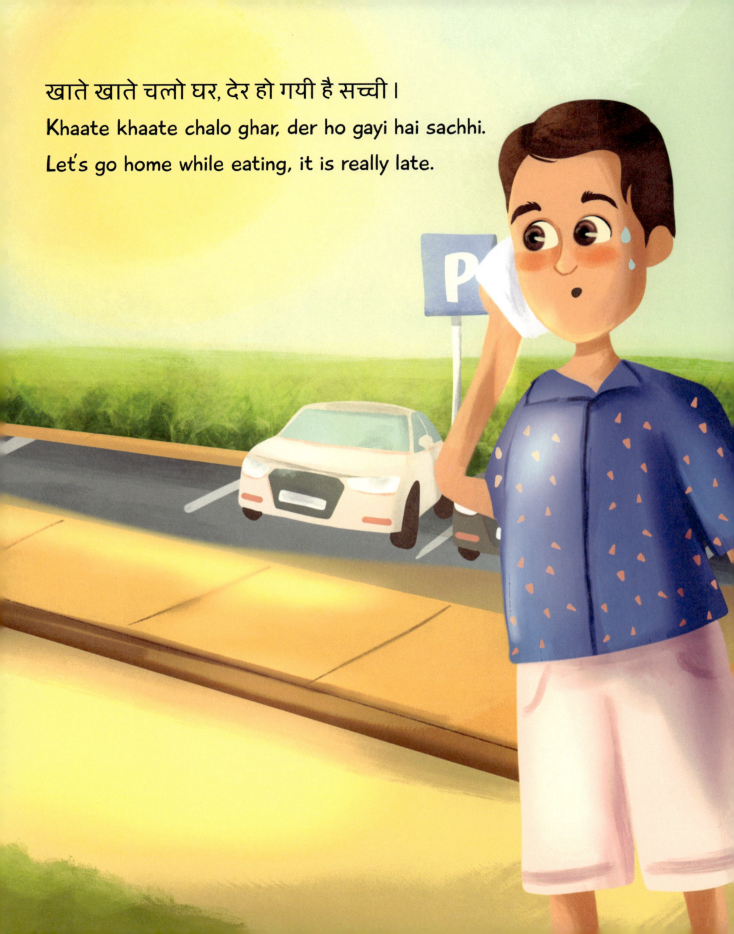

खाते खाते चलो घर, देर हो गयी है सच्ची।
Khaate khaate chalo ghar, der ho gayi hai sachhi.
Let's go home while eating, it is really late.

चलो अब नहा के साफ़ हो जाओ।
Chalo, ab naha ke saaf ho jao.
Let's go, take a bath now to get clean.

रात के खाने में है राजमा चावल की जोड़ी।
Raat ke khane mein hai rajma chaaval ki jodi.
Dinner has a combo of kidney beans and rice.

बाद में क्या मुझे खीर मिलेगी थोड़ी ?

Baad mein kya mujhe kheer milegi thodi?

Can I get a little rice pudding later?

खिलौनों से ज़्यादा, मेरी किताबें है मुझे प्यारी।

Khilaunon se zyada, meri kitaaben hai mujhe pyaari.

More than toys, I love my books.

यह आख़री किताब है, उसके बाद सोने की करो तैयारी।
Yeh aakhri kitaab hai, uske baad sone ki karo taiyaari.
This is the last book, after this get ready for bed.

चाँद और तारों से चमकती, अंधेरी रात है आई।

Chand aur taron se chamakti, andheri raat hai aayi.

The sparkling stars and moon are out with the dark night.

सपनों से भरी अखियों में, नए दिन की आशा है लाई ।
Sapnon se bhari akhiyon mein, naye din ki aasha hai layi.
In the eyes full of dreams, it brings hope for a new day.

हिंदी- अंग्रेज़ी शब्दकोष और खेल
Hindi- Angrezi Shabdakosh Aur Khel
Hindi- English Glossary and Games

क्या आप इंद्रधनुष को रंग के, नीचे लिखे सभी रंगों के नाम बता सकते हैं ?

Kya aap indradhanush ko rang ke, niche likhe sabhi rangon ke naam bata sakte hain?

Can you color the rainbow and name all the colors listed below?

रंग	Rang	Colors
लाल	Laal	Red
नारंगी	Narangi	Orange
पीला	Peela	Yellow
हरा	Hara	Green
नीला	Neela	Blue
बैंगनी	Baingani	Purple
काला	Kala	Black

क्या आप नीचे लिखी घड़ियों में सभी नंबर पढ़ सकते हैं?
Kya aap niche likhi ghadiyon mein sabhi nambar padh sakte hain?
Can you read all the numbers written in the clocks below?

गिनती/संख्या		Ginti/Sankhya	Numbers
१	एक	Ek	1
२	दो	Do	2
३	तीन	Teen	3
४	चार	Chaar	4
५	पांच	Paanch	5
६	छह	Che	6
७	सात	Saat	7
८	आठ	Aath	8
९	नौ	Nau	9
१०	दस	Dus	10
११	ग्यारह	Gyarah	11
१२	बारह	Barah	12

क्या आपने किताब पढ़ते समय इन विपरीत जोड़ियों पर ध्यान दिया ?
Kya aapne kitaab padte samay in vipareet jodiyon par dhyan diya?

Did you notice these pairs of opposites while reading the book?

दिन - Din - Day   रात - Raat - Night

सूरज - Suraj - Sun   चाँद - Chand - Moon

गरम - Garam - Hot   ठंडी - Thandi - Cold

जल्दी - Jaldi - Quickly   देर - Der - Late

इधर - Idhar - Here   उधर - Udhar - There

यहां - Yahan - Here   वहां - Wahan - There

थोड़ा - Thoda - Little   ज़्यादा - Zyada - More

About the Author

Anuja Mohla, DO is a physician who has turned author with her first book "Ek Naya Din". Born and brought up in New Delhi (India), Anuja immigrated to America as a teenager. Anuja realized the challenge her generation faces in teaching children about their heritage. Anuja found her passion for writing through her desire to empower her son to be multi-lingual. Having recognized that working parents have limited time, Anuja aspires to help young parents teach their native language to the next generation. In her spare time, she loves to cook and build on her love for Bollywood via movies, music, and dance.

About the Illustrator

Noor Alshalabi is a Jordan-based illustrator who started drawing ever since she learnt how to hold a pencil. After getting her BA in Visual Arts and Design, she pursued her dream of turning her imagination into reality through children's books. You can always find her with a cup of coffee, curled up with a good book, watching movies, playing with her pet bird, spending time with a friend, or going for a hike. Nature is both her source of inspiration and relaxation.

About the Editor

Aditi Wardhan Singh - An experienced editor of multicultural children's books, Aditi is a multi-award winning author of children's books and diverse books for parents. Featured on a number of broadcast networks and global publications, she is an authoritative voice on cultural sensitivity and empowerment.
Find her via RaisingWorldChildren.com

Made in United States
Troutdale, OR
01/26/2024

17197282R00019